STORES AND RETAIL SPACES | 10

From the Retail Design Institute and the Editors of *VMSD* magazine

ST MEDIA GROUP INTERNATIONAL

Cincinnati, Ohio

ISBN 10: 0-944094-63-5
ISBN 13: 978-0-944094-63-1

Published by:
ST Books, a division of ST Media Group International Inc.
11262 Cornell Park Drive | Cincinnati, Ohio 45242
P: 513-421-2050 | F: 513-744-6999 | E: books@stmediagroup.com
www.bookstore.stmediagroup.com

Distributed outside the U.S. to the book and art trade by:
Collins Design, an Imprint of HarperCollins Publishers
10 East 53rd Street | New York, NY 10022
www.harperdesigninternational.com

Book design by Kim Pegram, Art Director, *VMSD*
Competition winners written and edited by the Editors of *VMSD*
Additional descriptions written by Lauren Mang, Assistant Editor, *VMSD*
Book edited by Matthew Hall, Managing Editor, *Hospitality Style*

Printed in China
10 9 8 7 6 5 4 3 2 1

STORES AND RETAIL SPACES | 10

For 38 years, retailers, designers and architects from all over the
world have entered their finest projects in the *VMSD* International
Store Design Competition. Members of the Retail Design Institute
(formerly the Institute of Store Planners) gathered to determine the
best in retail design excellence from a variety of diverse submissions.

Here are those recognized winners from the *VMSD*/Retail Design
Institute International Store Design Competition judged in
November 2007, and published in *VMSD* in February 2008.

TABLE OF CONTENTS

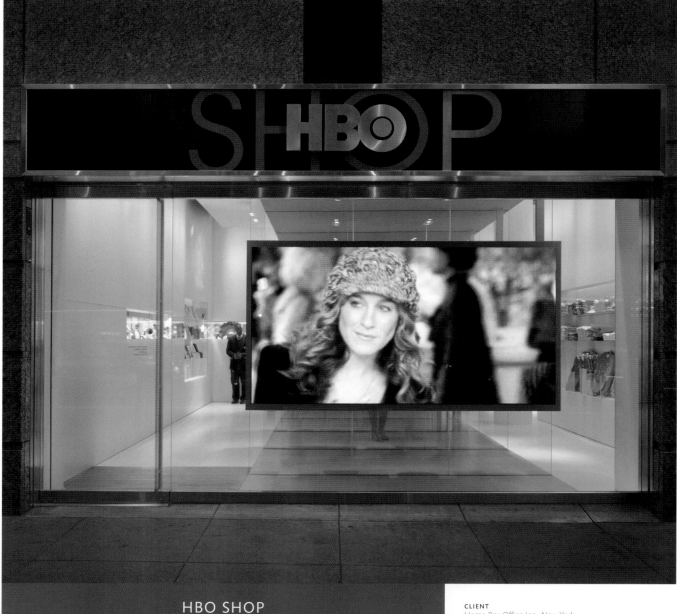

HBO SHOP

CLIENT
Home Box Office Inc., New York
DESIGN
Gensler, New York; Imaginary Forces, New York and
Hollywood, Calif.
AUDIO/VISUAL
Daktronics Inc., Brookings, S.D.
FIXTURES/MANNEQUINS/FORMS/PROPS AND DECORATIVES
Feature Factory, Toronto
LIGHTING
Color Kinetics Inc., Boston; Winona Lighting, Winona, Minn.;
Lutron Electronics Inc., Coopersburg, Pa.
SIGNAGE/GRAPHICS
Beyond Signs, Woodside, N.Y.
WALLCOVERINGS AND MATERIALS
Natali Glass Inc., Deer Park, N.Y.
PHOTOGRAPHY
Andrew Bordwin, Andrew Bordwin Studio Inc., New York

TV can really suck you in, and no one knows that better than HBO.
So the premium cable channel has brought that concept to life by
making the souvenir shop at its New York headquarters resemble an
oversized TV set.

It did so by creating an environment that immerses shoppers in
the premium cable channel's programs, including "The Sopranos" and
"Sex and the City." The store resembles an oversized TV set, featuring
merchandise on "floating" fixtures and a color-changing LED system.

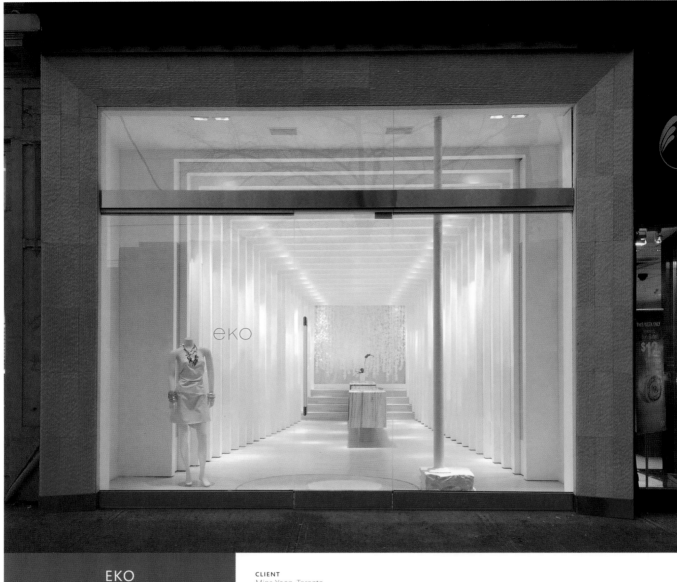

EKO

To rejuvenate its brand strategy, eko tapped Dialogue 38 to create an expanded retail space that elegantly reflects the innovative merchandise – contemporary jewelry by up-and-coming artisans worldwide. A floating marble display counter does double-duty as a cash counter.

Recessed vertical display cases create a sculptural backdrop that highlights the jewelry. Glass-encased displays framed by ribbed columns run the length of the 860-square-foot store. And a rear focal wall features a rotating installation by local artists.

CLIENT
Mina Yoon, Toronto

DESIGN/ARCHITECT
Dialogue 38, Toronto – Bennett Lo, principal

GENERAL CONTRACTOR
Canson Building Ltd., Toronto

OUTSIDE DESIGN CONSULTANT
Phoenix Electrical, Toronto (electrical)

ARTWALL
Japanese Paper Place, Toronto

FLOORING
Markham Flooring, Toronto

GLASS
Winners Glass, Toronto

LIGHTING
Cadalog Distribution, Toronto

MILLWORK
Bestway Millwork, Toronto

PAINT
Benjamin Moore Paint Co., Toronto

STONE
Satillo Imports, Toronto; Ciot Technica, Toronto

PHOTOGRAPHY
Eric Lau, Toronto

INNOVATION AWARD FOR CUTTING-EDGE CONCEPT

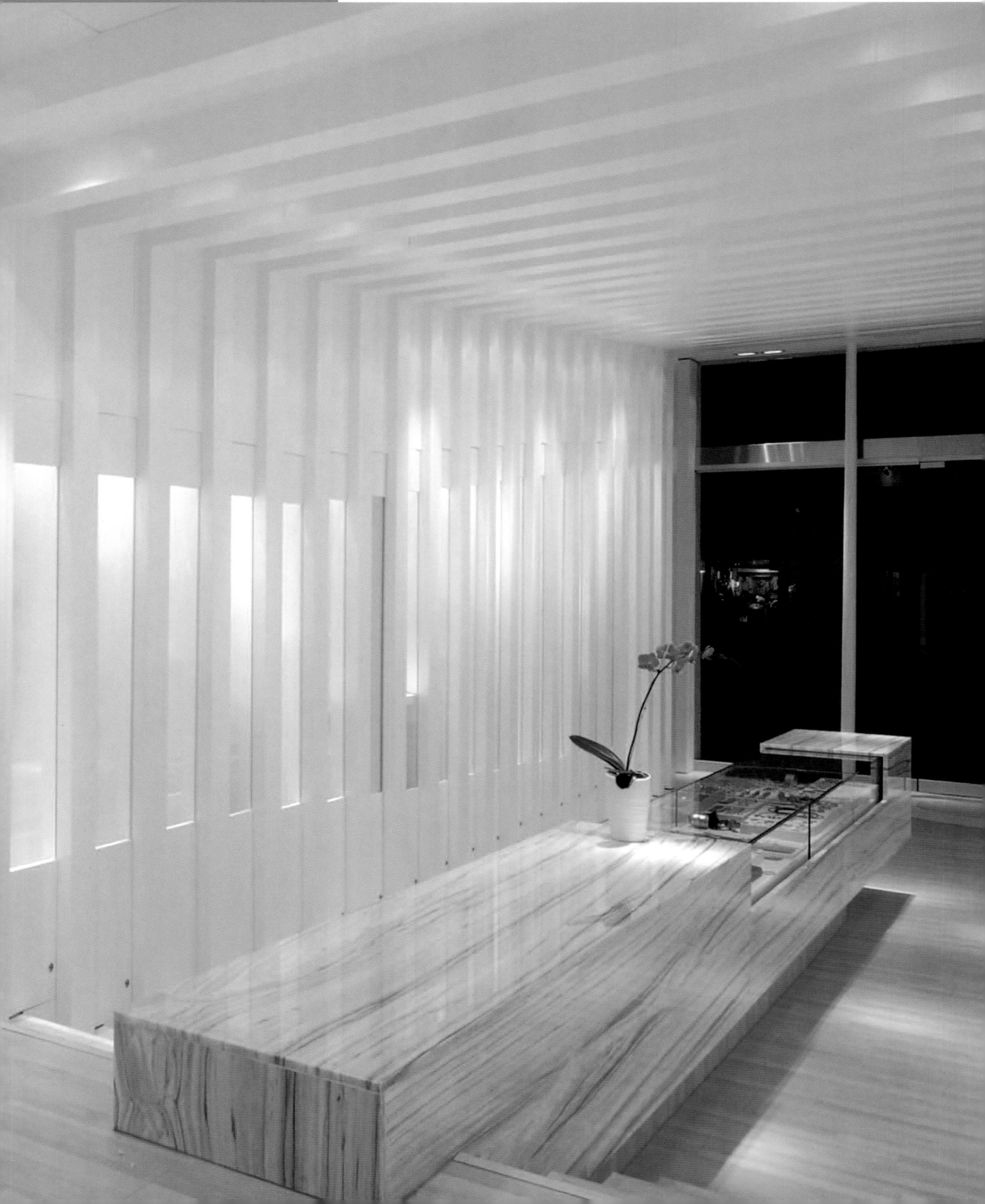

CAPEZIO

Burdifilek's new retail concept for Capezio elevates the brand from mainstream to cutting-edge with a deconstructivist aesthetic and a flair for the dramatic. Designers faced space challenges head-on by keeping product primarily on the store's perimeter.

Floor and seating areas in a modern Tokyo purple infuse color in the otherwise pristine-white space. And small, angular Lucite tables appear to grow organically around a single central seating area, which doubles as a feature art piece.

CLIENT
Markio Designs, Toronto – David Markowitz, CEO and president

DESIGN
burdifilek, Toronto – Paul Filek, managing partner; Diego Burdi, design director; Jeremy Mendonca, senior designer; Maria Kakarantza, senior CADD; Janice Kee-son and York Wu, junior designers; Alison Priestman, intermediate designer; Tom Yip, project manager

GENERAL CONTRACTOR
Structure Corp., Toronto

OUTSIDE DESIGN CONSULTANTS
MCW Consultants, Toronto (mechanical/electrical engineering); William Dewson Architect, Toronto (consulting architect); Blackwell Bowick, Toronto (structural engineering)

AUDIO/VISUAL
Bay Bloor Radio, Toronto

CARPET
Sullivan Source, Toronto

FURNITURE
Unique Store Fixtures, Toronto (custom glass tables)

LIGHTING
Litemore, Toronto

METALWORK
CB Metal, Toronto

MILLWORK
Luxe, Quebec City, Quebec

UPHOLSTERY
Maharam, Toronto; Creative Custom, Toronto

PHOTOGRAPHY
Ben Rahn, A Frame Inc., Toronto

SEIBU

Envisioned as a luxe launching point for regional designer brands and exclusive international lines, Seibu Jakarta's 108,000-square-foot store takes a retail-as-theater approach. A dramatic centrally located five-story etched-glass, chrome and mirror atrium boasts cantilevered stages that showcase custom displays and visual merchandising.

Each level is designed as a distinct space, while public areas are tied together with elegant, effusive displays and finishes. For example, finely detailed, layered installations blend textures, colors and patterns – including the Japanese cherry blossom – that draw on Seibu's Japanese heritage. And hand-carved and marble floors are accented by marble busts, carved statues and custom leather pieces handcrafted by local artisans.

CLIENT
PT. Panen Selaras Inti Buana, Jakarta, Indonesia

DESIGN FIRM
Callison, Seattle – Dawn Clark, principal-in-charge; Doug Shaw, project manager; Andy Thaemert, design director; Jeany Kim, Erik Mueller Ali, Nicole Bentley, design team

ARCHITECT
RTKL, Baltimore (building)

GENERAL CONTRACTOR
PT. Daya Indria Permai, Jakarta, Indonesia

INTERIOR CONTRACTORS
PT. Catur Griya Naradipa, Jakarta, Indonesia; PT. Andhikapura Perkasa, Jakarta, Indonesia; PT. Wahana Mega Hastakarya, Jakarta, Indonesia; Aljeff, Jakarta, Indonesia

LIGHTING
Lighting Design Alliance, Los Angeles; PT. LITAC, Jakarta, Indonesia

PHOTOGRAPHY
Stefanus Pakan, Jakarta, Indonesia

SHINSEGAE

A renovation of Shinsegae's 75-year-old, six-story store in Seoul, South Korea led to an elegant reinvention. A loft-like setting on the fourth and fifth floors appeals to younger consumers, with a 22-foot-wide, two-story platform creating a central focal point.

The sixth-floor VIP area boasts amenities such as lounge areas and a sculpture garden. And a suspended circular art piece comprised of strands of tiny acrylic forms provides a dramatic, luminous focal point overhead.

CLIENT
Shinsegae Co. Ltd., Seoul, South Korea – Yoon Soon-Young

DESIGN
RYA Design Consultancy, Dallas – Mike Wilkins and Chris Barriscale, co-creative directors; Kevin Roche, account director

ARCHITECT
Sam Woo Architects & Engineers, Seoul, South Korea

GENERAL CONTRACTOR
Shinsegae Engineering & Construction, Seoul, South Korea

OUTSIDE DESIGN CONSULTANTS
Keith Kosiba, Studio 321, San Francisco (lighting); Salty Design Group, Seoul, South Korea (graphics); Seven Continents, New York (visual merchandising)

CARPET
Scott Group, Dallas; Kesson Intl., Seoul, South Korea; Daehye Interiors & Architecture, Seoul, South Korea; Dooyang Construction Co., Ltd., Seoul, South Korea

FIXTURES
Faubion Associates, Dallas

FLOORING
Innovative Marble and Tile, Hauppauge, N.Y. (stone)

GILDED GLASS
American Burnish, Beacon, N.Y.

LIGHTING
Prescolite, Dallas; Indy Lighting, Des Plaines, Ill.; Bartco; Huntington Beach, Calif.

MILLWORK
Salty Design Group, Seoul, South Korea

PLASTER
Southwest Progressive Enterprises, Dallas

WALLCOVERINGS
Anya Larkin, New York; Silk Dynasty, San Jose, Calif.; Maharam, New York; Knoll, Dallas; Art People, New York; Carnegie, Rockville Center, N.Y.; Innovations, Dallas; DesignTex, Dallas; Donghia, Dallas

PHOTOGRAPHY
Courtesy of Shinsegae Co. Ltd., Seoul, Korea

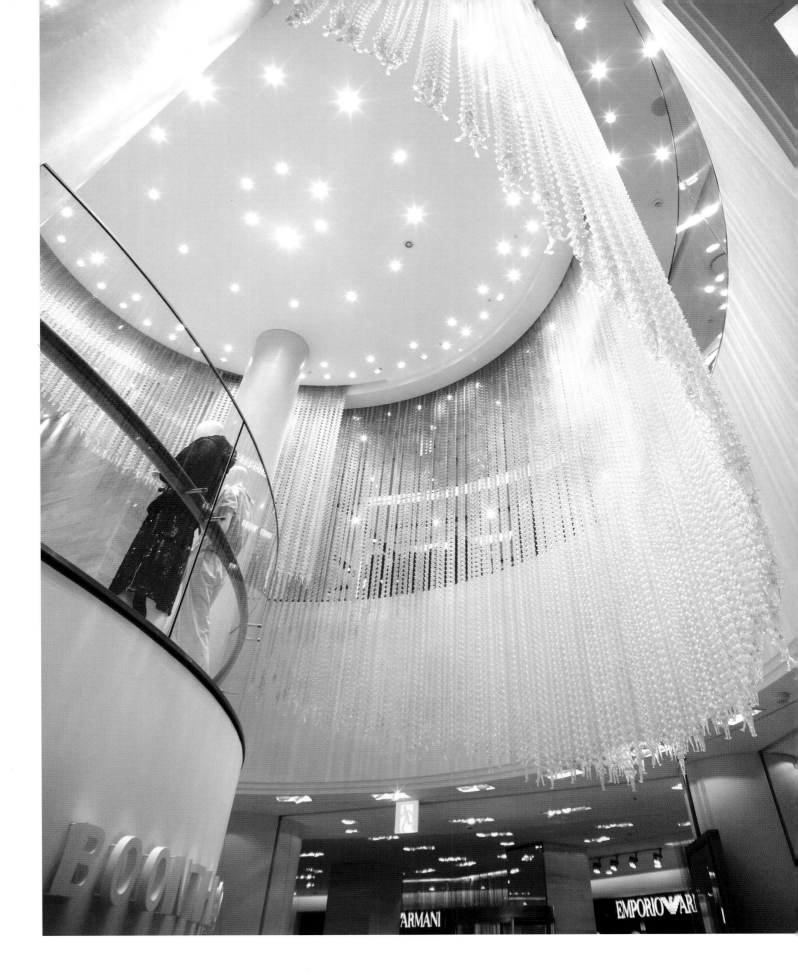

ROBINSONS DEPARTMENT STORE

For Robinsons' first store in Kuala Lumpur, Indonesia, the Singapore-based retailer repositioned itself as a contemporary yet romantic specialty department store. Taking inspiration from the mall name – The Garden – the store's circular ceiling details mimic ripples on a pond and create visual interest overhead. And in the handbag area, curved shelf-supports suggest bamboo poles.

Throughout the multilevel store, small details make a big impact. Elegant chandeliers denote the bedding area. Inset bookshelves lend masculinity to the men's department. And in the young women's department, illuminated square wall cutouts and mod furniture give a fashion-forward feel.

CLIENT
Robinsons & Co., Singapore

DESIGN
VMA Pte. Ltd., Singapore – Jose Maria Bustos, design director; Kingsmen Design PTE Ltd., Singapore – Gerald Tay

GENERAL CONTRACTOR
VMA Pte. Ltd., Singapore; Kingsmen Design Pte. Ltd., Singapore

FLOORING
Godfrey Hirst (S) Pte. Ltd., Singapore (carpet); Apex Stone Product Sdn. Bhd., Malaysia, Selangor (homogeneous tile); Ekowood M Sdn. Bhd., Malaysia, KL (timber flooring)

FURNITURE
Kingsmen Projects Pte. Ltd., Singapore

LAMINATE
TAK Products & Services Pte. Ltd., Singapore; EDL Pte. Ltd., Singapore; Lam Chuan Import-Export Pte. Ltd., Singapore

LIGHTING
Lumilux Design Pte. Ltd.

METALWORKS
Kejuruteraan Fong Hong Sdn. Bhd., Malaysia, JB; M&E Parsons Brinckerhoff Pte. Ltd., Singapore

WALLCOVERINGS
Goodrich Global Pte. Ltd., Singapore; Xessex Pte. Ltd., Singapore

PHOTOGRAPHY
Vernon Leow, Vital Images, Singapore

HUGO NICHOLSON

Canadian women's eveningwear and specialty department store, Hugo Nicholson, is a landmark in Toronto's Yorkville district. But after 15 years, the store was showing its age and its owners, Carole and Eleanor Rosenstein, were interested in a more international presence for the brand – a store where shoppers could find the likes of Prada, Gucci or Chanel.

To make the space suitable for everything from Galliano to Gaultier, designers at ICI Design & Construction (Toronto) updated the finishes, fixtures and flooring, improved the lighting and increased the visual merchandising all within the owners' guidelines not to abandon the charm of the original store.

The design is classic, yet contemporary, following Hugo Nicholson's elegant cream-and-black color scheme with hints of gold throughout the main space and silver accents in the private showroom and fitting room area. Swarovski crystal and pearlized wallcovering replace painted panel doors in the private showroom, adding sparkle to the area where expensive gowns are displayed. Lighting throughout the store was updated for better color-rendering and a warmer glow in the coves.

CLIENT
Hugo Nicholson, Toronto

DESIGN/GENERAL CONTRACTOR
ICI Design & Construction, Toronto – Noah Shopsowitz, executive vp, design

MARBLE TILE
AST Flooring, Toronto

GLASS
Albion Glass, Toronto

PLEXI BOXES AND SHELVES
Plexi Plus, Toronto

WALLCOVERING
Metro Wall Coverings and Fabrics, Toronto

LIGHTING
Juno Lighting Group, Brampton, Ont.

PAINTED METAL LETTERS
Studio 2 Custom, Toronto

MILLWORK
ICI Design & Construction, Toronto

PHOTOGRAPHY
Ben Rahn, A-Frame Inc., Toronto

TIMBERLAND IN MACY'S HERALD SQUARE

How do you install a brand-appropriate store-within-a-store concept for a rugged outdoor brand in an urban location? Very carefully. The Timberland footwear shop at Macy's Herald Square targets young metropolitan consumers through a design that blends a city vibe with a nod to the great outdoors.

Natural-finished walnut displays are backed by black acrylic. Recycled stone conveys Timberland's environmental philosophy. Black-and-white lifestyle photos of real people (rather than models) and images of the Manhattan skyline reinforce the product's down-to-earth attitude. And a community bulletin board encourages interaction by allowing customers to post local concerts and events.

CLIENT
Macy's Herald Square, New York

DESIGN
The Timberland Co., Stratham, N.H. – Bevan Bloemendaal, senior director, global creative services; David Curtis, senior manager, environments group; Jean Wood, fixturing manager; Amy Tauchert, senior visual merchandising manager; Janice Massey, store planning and events

ARCHITECT
LODA, Montreal

GENERAL CONTRACTOR
Dynamic Resources, New York

OUTSIDE DESIGN CONSULTANTS
Synnott Imaging, Plainfield, Conn. (signage/graphics); Dynamic Resources (installation)

FIXTURES
Fleetwood Industries, Leesport, Pa.

FLOORING
Architectural Systems Inc., New York

GRAPHICS
Synnott Imaging, Plainfield, Conn.

LIGHTING
Lido Lighting, Deer Park, N.Y.

PHOTOGRAPHY
Mark Steele, Mark Steele Photography, Columbus, Ohio

STYLED BY ME™ BARBIE®

Located at FAO Schwarz's Fifth Avenue store, this customized retail experience lets girls create their own Barbie® dolls at interactive styling stations and then watch their creations strut on a mechanized runway. Monitors announce the dolls, which float on frosted-acrylic panels to the beat of music, while LEDs flash and "cameras" click. Creamy whites, pinks and silvers lend a soft, neutral backdrop for the colorful merchandise and packaging and add a feminine contrast to the high-tech styling stations.

CLIENT/DESIGN
Mattel Inc., El Segundo, Calif. – Richard Dickson, senior vice president of marketing, media and entertainment, worldwide; Kim Helgeson, visual merchandising manager

OUTSIDE DESIGN CONSULTANTS
Six Foot Studio, Houston (interactive software development); Technifex, Valencia, Calif. (runway mechanical design)

AUDIO/VISUAL
AVR Inc., Danbury, Conn.

FIXTURES
Greneker Solutions, Los Angeles; Creative Forces, Monrovia, Calif.; Spark Retail Solutions, Huntington Beach, Calif.

FLOORING
Amtico Intl., Atlanta

LIGHTING
Royal Lighting Inc., New York (chandelier)

MANNEQUINS/FORMS
Greneker Solutions, Los Angeles

PROPS AND DECORATIVES
Mattel Inc., El Segundo, Calif.

SIGNAGE/GRAPHICS
Spark Retail Solutions, Huntington Beach, Calif.

PHOTOGRAPHY
John Fleck, Indianapolis

3RD NATURE

Watt International (Toronto) helped develop the concept and design for 3rd Nature – a retail model geared toward the passionate performance-cycling enthusiast. Set in a gallery-like space where the product is hero, the store offers nutrients and refreshments for those making a pit stop and a service area for those in need of a quick repair.

Precision components are showcased in glass display cases, frames are displayed on rolling racks, and apparel and accessories are housed on modular fixtures. A frame-fitting area allows for bike customization or fitness activities (yoga, spinning). And wall graphics appeal to customers' healthy attitude and passion for pedals.

CLIENT
Michael Kastner and Michael McTigue, Teaneck, N.J.

DESIGN
Watt International, Toronto – Jean Paul Morresi, executive creative director; Brian Dyches, vice president, global insight + strategy; Matt DeAbreu, senior illustrator/designer; Vicky Chin, designer; Debbie Marks, senior graphic designer; Liliana Saavedra, account manager

FIXTURES
ALU, Toronto

FIXTURES/CABINETRY
David Leitz Custom Woodworking, Linden, N.J.

GRAPHICS/CUSTOM WALLCOVERINGS
PMG Ad Group, Darien, Conn.

MILLWORK
Sullivan Source, Toronto

SEATING UPHOLSTERY
Maharam, Toronto

PHOTOGRAPHY
David Demarest, PMG AD Group, Darien, Conn.

"Plunge boldly into the thick of life, and seize it where you will, it is always inte

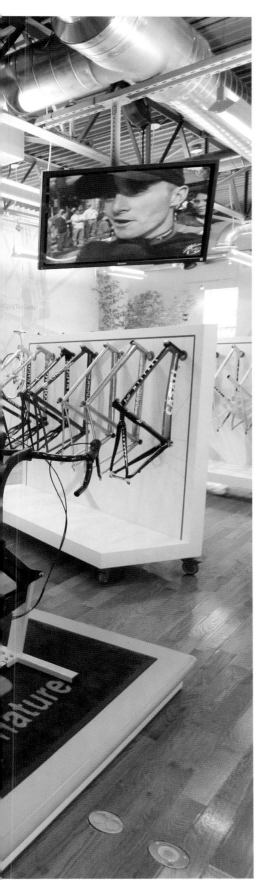

MASKA

Designed to keep pace with Zara and
H&M, the new 2,000-square-foot Maska
store draws shoppers in from the get-go,
with a storefront display of mannequins in a
fluorescent, patterned-acrylic frame.

Inside, the predominantly white store
is punctuated with fuchsia accents and
periodic bold damask wallcoverings. Playful
feature tables are used in lieu of metal racks,
a waterfall chandelier brings a decidedly
feminine touch, and a rear graphic wall adds
a dramatic focal point.

CLIENT
Maska, Montreal

DESIGN
Ruscio Studio Inc., Montreal – Robert Ruscio, president and
principal designer; Audrey Ferron, designer

GENERAL CONTRACTOR
DAMA Construction, Dorval, Que.

FLOORING
Italbec Intl., Montreal

GRAPHICS
Vivimar Creations, St.-Laurent, Que.

LAMINATES
Octopus, Laval, Que.; Oberflex, Brooklyn, N.Y.; Nevamar, St.
Laurent, Que.

LIGHTING
Juno Lighting, Sainte-Therese, Que.; Artcraft Lighting, Anjou,
Que. (chandelier)

MANNEQUINS
Adco, Saint-Hubert, Que.

METAL
Roy Metal Inc., Saint-Francois de Montmagny, Que.

MOLDING
Bois Expansion, Montreal

WALLCOVERINGS
Crown Wallpaper, Westmount, Que.

PHOTOGRAPHY
Robert Ruscio, Montreal

DOLPHIN CAY

Dolphin Cay is a new, 11-acre, state-of-the-art dolphin rescue and education center located at Atlantis, Paradise Island, the Bahamas. The habitat was created for 17 dolphins that previously resided at the Marine Life Oceanarium in Gulfport, Miss., which was destroyed by Hurricane Katrina. The dolphins' new home is an interactive haven, where resort guests can swim and interact with dolphins in the 7-million-gallon artificial habitat.

When the swimmers emerge from their dolphin adventure, they enter a space Bada-Crema Design Consultants envisioned as a simulation of their experience. Two types of flat-screen interfaces form a key component of the welcome. First, a pair of wall-mounted 40-inch plasma screens at the left of the entrance present "teaser" footage of previous groups' visits. Bada-Crema specified a textured aqua blue solid surface for the counter top, incorporating several Caribbean water colors into glass panels along the front face. These shimmering shades and textures were echoed throughout the roughly circular shopping space, which repeats graceful curves that mirror the shapes of the dolphin sculptures suspended overhead.

CLIENT, GENERAL CONTRACTOR AND SIGNAGE/GRAPHICS
Kerzner Intl., Atlantis, Paradise Island, the Bahamas

DESIGN AND LIGHTING
Launch by Design, a div. of Bada-Crema Design Consultants Ltd., Toronto – Ann Bada-Crema, president

AUDIO/VISUAL
Technomedia Solutions LLC, Orlando

FLOORING
Stone Tile, Toronto

MILLWORK
All Wood Fine Interiors Ltd., Toronto

SUSPENDED DOLPHINS
Zoran Worldwide, Marietta, Ga.

PHOTOGRAPHY
Interior Images, a div. of Richard Johnson Photography, Toronto

INNOVATION AWARD FOR LIGHTING

SONY ERICSSON

Sony Ericsson's first store features a compelling, no-pressure, non-technical environment intended to attract a broad range of consumers. A floor-to-ceiling glass storefront and bright, color-changing fascia in the brand's signature color palette (purple, red and green) add visual impact from the get-go.

Inside, ergonomic forms, vibrant colors and a light aesthetic reflect the design philosophy of the Japanese/Swedish brand. For example, the store's architectural focal point is the infinity bar – a white, sculpted oval display where customers can sample and learn more about the products. And perimeter merchandising is delineated by colorful displays that are inset, angled and illuminated from above and below.

CLIENT
Sony Ericsson, London – Salv D'Angelo, retail marketing director, global marketing

DESIGN
Checkland Kindleysides, Leicester, U.K. – Steve Pearce, account director; Tony Bell, project manager; Joe Evans, Clive Hunt, and Laura Dixon, interior designers; Carl Murch, graphics

GENERAL CONTRACTOR
Oakwood Shopfitting, Andover, U.K.

AC Howvale, Nottingham, U.K.

AUDIO/VISUAL
Sony Corp., New York (supplier); Bits, Reading, U.K. (installer)

ELECTRIC
McConnells, Newark, U.K.

FURNITURE
Checkland Kendleysides, Leicester, U.K.

HANDSET SECURITY
Stacey Security, Cheshire, U.K.

LIGHTING
Tritech, Birmingham, U.K. (LEDs); Modular Lighting, London (general)

SIGNAGE
Sovereign Signs Hull, Humberside, U.K.

PHOTOGRAPHY
Keith Parry, London

AT&T EXPERIENCE STORE

Designed to tell the story of AT&T and Cingular's brand evolution – while offering a one-stop shop for communications products and home entertainment services – the 5000-square-foot AT&T Experience Store incorporates elements of both brands. Sleek blue graphics, streamlined fixtures and finishes, and a clearly defined floor plan integrate Cingular's "Raising the Bar" brand with AT&T's signature blue.

Six distinct experience zones are delineated with signage and ceiling/flooring cues. And merchandise stations allow customers to test-drive everything from XM Satellite Radio on Bluetooth headphones to high-definition home entertainment devices. Ten more stores will open nationwide to make communications and entertainment purchases fun rather than frightening.

CLIENT
AT&T, San Antonio

DESIGN
Callison, Seattle – Eric Lagerberg, principal; Alex Shapleigh, design director; Elaine Schneider, project manager; Michael Riggs, Peiter Buick and Alexandra Ramsden, design team

ARCHITECT OF RECORD
Oculus Inc., St. Louis

GENERAL CONTRACTOR
Spec-Built, Inc., Carrollton, Texas

OUTSIDE DESIGN CONSULTANT
Sean O'Conner Associates, Philadelphia (lighting)

FIXTURES
RCS Retail Interiors, Milwaukee

TECHNOLOGY
IBM Global Services/Business Consulting Services, multiple U.S. locations

PHOTOGRAPHY
Chris Eden, Callison, Seattle

Home TV Entertainment

UMBRA

Umbra, a hip housewares manufacturer, wanted its new concept store in Toronto to reflect the company's design-driven DNA. To help make that statement, the two-level building was wrapped in 300 translucent pink slats. The panels are spaced 6 inches apart, which provides passersby with tantalizing glimpses into the store's sleek, white minimalist interior.

CLIENT
Umbra, Toronto – Les Mandelbaum, president

DESIGN
figure3, Toronto – Allan Guinan and Christopher Wright, partners, Ralph Dopping, senior team lead; Steve Tsai, Rob Jarschke, Colin Gran and Marion Juton, project designers

ARCHITECT
Kohn Shnier, Toronto – John Shnier, partner

GENERAL CONTRACTOR
Urbacon, Toronto

FLOORING
Maxxon, Hamel, Minn.; Johnsonite, Chagrin Falls, Ohio; Interface, Toronto

EXIT

U
umbra

INNOVATION AWARD FOR EXTERIOR

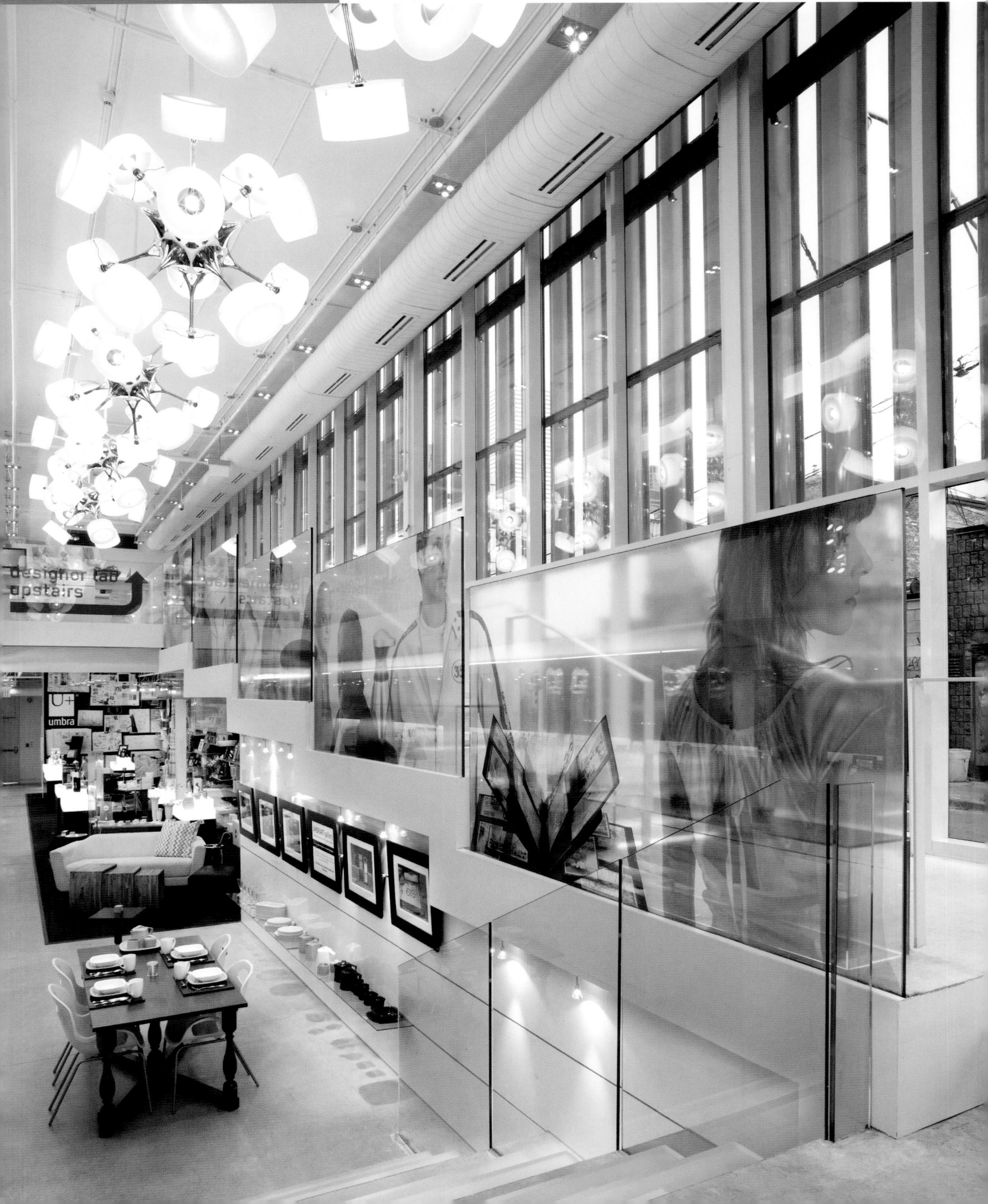
designer lab
upstairs
U+
umbra

CHICAGO BOTANIC GARDEN SHOP

The Chicago Botanic Garden bills itself as "the premier teaching garden in the country," owing to its expertise in botany science and conservation education. When renovating the complex's 3700-square-foot retail store, the garden's operators sought to create an environment that reinforced that expertise, while also being more engaging and visitor-friendly.

Hired to work with the in-house team in meeting those objectives was Charles Sparks + Co., which has spiffed up the retail spaces for several other high-profile museums and attractions, including the Nelson Atkins Museum of Art and the Lincoln Park Zoo. In updating the Botanic Garden store, designers infused the space with natural finishes and installed a central esplanade with nested tables down its center. Each table grouping contains related products that tell a different "story," such as "How to create that classic English garden look."

CLIENT
Chicago Botanic Garden, Glencoe, Ill. – Barbara Whitney Carr, president and ceo; Sophia Siskel, vp, visitor operations; William Brown, vp, facilities and planning; Kris Jarantoski, evp and director; Barbara Voss, store manager; Zina Castanuela, design manager

DESIGN
Charles Sparks + Co., Westchester, Ill. – Charles Sparks, designer; Stan Weisbrod, project manager; Rachel Mikolajczyk, director, resource studio; Stephanie Arakawa-Moore, director, graphic communications

ARCHITECT
SJW & Associates, Westchester, Ill.

CONSTRUCTION MANAGEMENT
Featherstone Inc., Downers Grove, Ill.

OUTSIDE CONSULTANTS
Brown & Associates Inc., Lincolnwood, Ill. (project management); Grumman/Butkus Associates, Evanston, Ill. (MP engineer); Dickerson Engineering, Niles, Ill. (electrical engineer)

AREA RUGS
Ombre Inc., Evanston, Ill.

FABRICS
Knoll Textiles, Chicago; Nathan Chapin Ltd., Chicago

FIXTURES
Custom Commercial Environments, Lincolnshire, Ill.

GLASS
Twin City Creative Mirror, Burnsville, Minn.; Griffin Resource Group, Chicago

MATERIALS
Architectural Systems Inc., New York; 3form, New Lenox, Ill.

PAINTS
Benjamin Moore, Melrose Park, Ill.

PLASTIC LAMINATES
Parkwood Chicago, Wheeling, Ill.; Wilsonart Intl. Inc., Evanston, Ill.; Formica Corp., Cincinnati

WALLCOVERINGS
Thybony Wallcoverings, Chicago

WOOD
R.S. Bacon Veneer, Burr Ridge, Ill.

PHOTOGRAPHY
Charlie Mayer Photography, Oak Park, Ill.

"*I do not understand how anyone can live without some small place of enchantment to turn to.*"
- marjorie kinnan rawlings

Helianthus annuus SUNFLOWER ❧ *Hemerocallis flava* YELLOW DAYLILY ❧ *Hibiscus moscheutos* ROSE MALLOW ❧ *Hydrangea arborescens* SMOOTH HYDRANGEA ❧ *Ipom*

INNOVATION AWARD FOR FINISHES

SAMSUNG ELECTRONICS

Samsung is South Korea's largest electronics company and one of the world's biggest manufacturers of DVD players, big-screen televisions, computers and the like. For its latest retail strategy, the brand is launching flagships and concept shops in major markets across the world.

The first phase of its global initiative is the 3700-square-foot prototype on London's Tottenham Court Road. To provide a unified and recognizable brand image throughout the world, the design firm fashioned a concept with a consistent brand color palette and a modern design.

Interactivity begins right at the shop's entrance with a communal table called the Imagine Bar where customers can try out the latest products. Upstairs is a mock living room, complete with modern furnishings and a Samsung flat screen.

Bright graphics with phrases such as "pure style" and "vivid realism" aim to reinforce the brand's identity, as does the space's strong color statement.

CLIENT
Samsung Electronics, Global Marketing Operations, Seoul, Korea; Samsung UK, Chertsey, Surrey, U.K.; Cheil Communications, Seoul, Korea

DESIGN
Lippincott, New York -- Randall Stone, senior partner; Ryan Kovalak, senior associate; Alissa Tribelli, associate; Michael Milligan, associate; Jung Shin, designer

ARCHITECT
Angus Pong Architecture, London

GENERAL CONTRACTOR
Portview, Belfast, Ireland

OUTSIDE DESIGN CONSULTANTS
Hekman Badhwar Global Partnership, Toronto (construction management)

CEILINGS
Barrisol USA, Cleveland

FIXTURES
Umdasch Shop Concept, Amstetten, Austria; DNS Display Industries Inc., Toronto

FLOORING
Byrock, London

CARPET
Bentley Prince Street, City of Industry, Calif.

FURNITURE
Derin, London; SCP, London; Angela Adams, Portland, Maine

UPHOLSTERY
Maharam, New York; Cortina Leather, New York

LIGHTING
JCC Lighting, West Sussex, U.K.

WALLCOVERING/MATERIALS
Portland Color, Portland, Maine; DuPont, Wilmington, Del.

COLORED GLASS
Vanceva, St. Louis

PHOTOGRAPHY
Lippincott, New York

MARTIN + OSA

Martin + Osa is a new brand concept that takes inspiration from real-life adventurers Martin and Osa Johnson. Design details reflect the attitude of the target consumer: active-minded, adventure-seeking 25- to 40-year-olds.

Large cypress plank doors at the entrance are used in lieu of glass. A cypress-lined lounge with a ping-pong table invites customers to literally come inside and play. Cypress floor and rafters add warmth underfoot and overhead. A wall-mounted memory wall of 1,000 black-and-white adventure photos taken by the store's staff. And a gathering table, seating nook and two "cabins" showcase products in a communal fashion.

CLIENT
American Eagle Outfitters, Pittsburgh – Chuck Chupein, COO; Deb McKeand, director, creative services

DESIGN/ARCHITECTURE
Michael Neumann Architecture LLC, New York – Michael Neumann, principal; Jeff Rudy, project manager; Talin Rudy, Vivian Prunner, and Daniel Gillen, project team

GENERAL CONTRACTOR
Commercial Construction Management, Upper Darby, Pa.

OUTSIDE DESIGN CONSULTANT
Johnson Schwinghammer Lighting Consultants, New York (lighting)

AUDIO/VISUAL
PlayNetwork, Redmond, Wash.

FIXTURES
Amuneal Manufacturing, Philadelphia

FLOORING
Stone Source, New York

LIGHTING
Nippo, Iselin, N.J.; Litelab, Buffalo, N.Y.; Chris Lehrecke Pendants, Bangall, N.Y.

MEMORY WALL
Daniel Gillen, Michael Neumann Architecture, New York

PHOTOGRAPHY
Sharon Risedorph, San Francisco

SAQ SÉLECTION

The design for the 8200-square-foot SAQ Sélection grew out of a marketing study that revealed consumers wanted more oenological savvy to make informed purchasing decisions. To this end, a discovery zone at the front of the store offers free wine tasting, wine recommendations by price range and suggestions for wine/food pairings.

Simple slate-gray fixtures, a clear visual communication system, as well as soft lighting, wood floors and wall paneling combine to create a warm, sophisticated atmosphere.

CLIENT
Société des Alcools du Québec, Montreal – Daniel Aumont, director, interior design and engineering; Chantale St-Pierre, senior director, marketing

DESIGN
Ædifica, Montreal – Michel Dubuc, architect, partner in charge; Jeanne-Pierre Généreux, architect, partner in charge of design; Stéphane Bernier, senior designer/interior design; Nicolas Côté, senior designer/furniture; Julie Larouche, junior designer; Jean-Yves Rouleau and team, plans and specifications

SidLee, Montreal – Jean-François Bouchard, CEO; Hélène Godin, creative director; Isabelle D'Astous, art director; Catherine Laporte, designer; Régine Buès, coordinator; Peter Pigeon, production director; Graphique M&H, graphic design

ARCHITECT
Ædifica Inc., Montreal

GENERAL CONTRACTOR
Procam, Boucherville, Que.

CEILING
Armstrong World Industries Inc., Lancaster, Pa.

FIXTURES
Étalex, Montreal

FLOORING
Arteca Flooring, Atlanta

FURNITURE
Arold/Chaises Sylco, St-Pie, Que.

LIGHTING
Juno Lighting, Des Plaines, Ill.

MILLWORK
Ébénisterie René Daigle, Quebec City, Que.

SIGNAGE/GRAPHICS
SidLee, Montreal; CPS Serigraphie, Quebec City, Que.; Transworld, Montreal

WALLCOVERINGS
CPS Serigraphie, Quebec City, Que.

WINE SERVING SYSTEM
Enomatic, Chianti, Italy

PHOTOGRAPHY
Michel Tremblay, Montreal, and André Rider, Montreal

THE NEW WORLD OF COCA-COLA

Designed as the exit retail for the attraction of the same name – and as the flagship for a new global retail concept – The New World of Coca-Cola appeals to a global community of Coke fans while reaching out to trendsetters and style leaders.

A circular floor pattern features "pavilions" that highlight unique product offerings. An affordable custom fixturing system offers multiple display options for rollouts. And a circular ceiling element and graphics create visual interest overhead.

CLIENT
Coca-Cola, Atlanta – Linda Conrad, general manager, Coca-Cola, retail and attractions; Patrick Kells, director of commercialization, worldwide licensing; Kelly Kozel, senior design manager, brand/retail stores; David MacConnie, visual manager, retail and attractions; Nathan Facteau, assistant creative manager, retail attractions

DESIGN
Pompei A.D. LLC, New York – Ron Pompei, founder and creative director; Colin Brice, executive director, architecture and design; Scott Faucheux, senior project manager; Aylin Cinarli and David Ostow, project managers; Drew Lytle, assistant project manager; Monte Antrim, graphic designer

ARCHITECT
Rosser Intl., Atlanta

GENERAL CONTRACTORS
Holder Construction Co., Atlanta; Manhattan Construction Co., Atlanta; C.D. Moody Construction Co., Lithonia, Ga.

OUTSIDE DESIGN CONSULTANTS
Jones Lang LaSalle, Atlanta (program manager); Johnson Light Studio, New York (lighting)

AUDIO/VISUAL
DMX Music, Austin, Texas; Electrosonic Systems Inc., Orlando

FIXTURES
Jon Glanz Associates, Ho-Ho-Kus, N.J.; MG Concepts, Central Islip, N.Y.; Sincerely International, Hong Kong

FLOORING
Smith & Fong Plyboo, San Francisco; Ecostone, Calgary; Commercial Flooring Services/HPI, Inc., Fayetteville, GA

FURNITURE
Quinze & Milan, Bronx, N.Y.

LIGHTING
Cleveland Electric Co., Atlanta; Uptime Electric Co., Lithonia, Ga.

MANNEQUINS/FORMS
Goldsmith, Inc., New York; Seven Continents, Toronto

PROPS AND DECORATIVES
Seven Continents, Toronto; Greneker Solutions, Los Angeles; Visual Designs and Sources, Valrico, Calif.; RAP, Cudahy, Calif.; Creative Design and Development, Sanford, Fla.; JG Associates, Ho-Ho-Kus, N.J.

SIGNAGE/GRAPHICS
Seven Continents, Toronto; Promoworks, Lawrenceville, Ga.

WALLCOVERINGS AND MATERIALS
Designers Plastics, Clearwater, Fla.

PHOTOGRAPHY
Robert d'Addona, New York

M&M'S WORLD NEW YORK

CLIENT
Mars Retail Group, Henderson, Nev. – John Haugh, president; Blair Ford, vice president, retail; John Murray, vice president, services and finance; Scott Mogren, vice president, personnel and organization; Cindy Wix Ingling, director, store operations; Jennifer Gudgel, director, merchandise; Brian McNally, director, product development; Lanita Isler, director, marketing; Christopher Lossing, real estate contract and project manager

DESIGN
Chute Gerdeman, Columbus, Ohio – Dennis Gerdeman, principal; Brian Shafley, president and creative director; Wendy Johnson, executive vice president, account management; Bess Anderson, director, visual strategy; Steve Boreman, senior designer, brand communications; Steve Pottschmidt, director, design development; Andy Jagger, designer, design development; Susan Siewny, director, graphic production; Steve Johnson and George Waite, designers, graphic production

DESIGN ARCHITECT
CG Architecture, Columbus, Ohio

CONSULTING ARCHITECT
Jerome S. Gillman, New York

CONSTRUCTION MANAGEMENT
Premier Management Alliance, Tustin, Calif.

GENERAL CONTRACTOR
Mackenzie Keck Inc., Hackettstown, N.J.

OUTSIDE DESIGN CONSULTANTS
Illuminating Concepts, Farmington Hills, Mich. (lighting); M-Retail, Westerville, Ohio (MEP engineer); Rosenwasser/Grossman, New York (structural engineer); R. Scott Lewis, New Canaan, Conn. (exterior signage structural engineer); Winston & Co., Inc., Teaneck, N.J. (LED/exterior signage); VDA, Livingston, N.J. (vertical transportation systems); Consentini Associates, New York (fire alarm and protection systems)

AUDIO/VISUAL
Dixon Entertainment Arts, Henderson, Nev

FABRICS AND BEADS
Moss, Belfast, Maine; ShimmerScreen, Mt. Vernon, N.Y.

FIXTURES
Seven Continents, Toronto; Group DKG, Toronto

LIGHTING
Weidenbach-Brown, Hawthorne, N.Y. (show control, special fffects); Show and Tell, New York; Excel Media, New York

MILLWORK
Universal Custom Display, Elk Grove, Calif.; Total Display Services, Binghamton, N.Y.

RETAIL HARDWARE
Capitol Hardware, Niles, Mich.

SCENIC AND SCULPTURE
Symmetry Products Group, Lincoln, R.I.; Skyline Design, Chicago

SIGNAGE/GRAPHICS
Superior Graphics & Signage, Jackson, N.J. (interior signage); Broadway National, Ronkonkoma, N.Y.; LED Spectrum, Farmingdale, N.Y. (exterior signage); D3 LED, Union City, N.J.; Landmark, New York; Show and Tell, New York

VISUAL
Seven Continents, Toronto; ALU, New York; Storeworks, Inc., Eden Prairie, Minn.; Minard Bernier Import Export, Toronto; Acrylicon, Columbus, Ohio

PHOTOGRAPHY
Mark Steele Photography, Columbus, Ohio

Rather than compete with its high-profile location – New York's Times Square – the M&M's World store takes inspiration from it. Housed in a 25,000-square-foot, three-level glass box, the megastore features two massive LED screens mounted on the exterior and M&M's Brand Characters with a New York flair inside.

Blue Fever takes cues from "Saturday Night Fever" in a Swarovski crystal-encrusted white leisure suit. A 17-foot-tall Green M&M mimics the Statue of Liberty, while Red is a high-rise window washer. Other features include a subway-inspired ceiling graphic and illuminated pillars that are choreographed to change color simultaneously with the exterior signage.

BASS PRO SHOPS SPORTSMAN'S CENTER

The new Bass Pro Shops Sportsman's Center in Miami is a living monument to Florida's fishing, boating and marina life. The theme of underwater exploration is conveyed through a sunken-ship display that doubles as a 19,000-gallon saltwater aquarium.

Murals of the Everglades, historic Stiltsville and underwater life reinforce the oceanic feel. And the fishing-counter design pays homage to Biscayne Bay houses that stand on pilings in shallow water.

CLIENT
Bass Pro Shops, Inc., Springfield, Mo.

DESIGN
Bass Pro Shops Inc. Architects, Springfield, Mo. – Tom Jowett, vice president, design and development; Sean Easter, vice president of construction; Mart Tuttle, director of architecture; George Carameros, director of merchandise presentation and imagery; Lenny Clark, senior technical designer; Julie Dowden, project designer; Glennon Scheid, interior project manager; Bill Stidham, project manager/quality manager; Monica Matthias, interior project manager, fixtures and signage; Rick Collins, taxidermy; Ed Dinkins, vice president of merchandising; Pam Honeycutt, purchasing agent/design coordinator

ARCHITECT
Mike Hughes Architects, Tulsa, Okla.

GENERAL CONTRACTOR
VCC, Irving, Texas

OUTSIDE DESIGN CONSULTANTS
SWT Design, St. Louis (landscape architect); Cost of Wisconsin, Jackson, Wis. (aquarium); Hoss & Brown, Lawrence, Kan. (electrical and mechanical engineering); Interior Planning Consultants, Springfield, Mo. (interiors); Mettemeyer Engineering, Springfield, Mo. (structural engineering)

BAHAMA-STYLE SHUTTERS
Taylored Services Inc., Marathon, Fla.; Florida Storm Protection Unlimited, Boynton Beach, Fla.

CARPET
Mohawk Carpet & Affiliates, Calhoun, Ga.

CERAMIC TILE
Millennium Marble and Tile Inc., Pembroke Park, Fla.

COLUMN LOG WRAPS
Nautical Furnishings, Ft. Lauderdale, Fla.

DOORS, FRAMES, HARDWARE
LaForce Inc., Vernon Hills, Ill.

EQUIPMENT INSTALLATION
Summit Installation LLC, Brooks, Ky.

EXTERIOR FINISH SYSTEM
Prestige Stucco Inc., Cumming, Ga.

FIXTURES
Bass Pro Fabrication Shop, Nixa, Mo.; TJ Hale & Co., Menomonee Falls, Wis.; Lozier, St. Peters, Mo.; Rocky Creek, Stephenville, Texas;

FLAGSTONE
Masonry Central Broward Construction, Ft. Lauderdale, Fla.

FURNITURE
Smith & Hawken, Novato, Calif.

GRAPHICS
Garage Graphics, Springfield, Mo.; Design Image, St. Louis; Bass Lithocolor Inc., Springfield, Mo.; Novacolor, St. Louis

IMAGERY
Framing PFI Artworks, Kansas City, Kan.

LIGHTING
City Lighting, Kansas City, Mo.; PCX Corp., Clayton, N.C.

LANDSCAPING AND IRRIGATION
AllGreen Nursery Inc., Princeton, Fla.

MURALS
Bob Sopchick, York, Pa.; Chad Bryan, Atlanta; Biruta Hansen, Liverpool, Pa.; Dennis Burkart, Wrightsville, Pa.; John Whytock, Joshua Tree, Calif.

PAINT
Service Painting Corp., Orlando

PROPS AND DECORATIVES
Roadside Rustics, Eureka Springs, Ark.

TILE
Unique Tile Ltd., Nixa, Mo.

PHOTOGRAPHY
Janell Willis, Bass Pro Shops, Springfield, Mo.

THE MOBILE LOUNGE

The Mobile Lounge offers high-tech products in an Internet café environment. Customers can relax in the lounge or use individual touchscreen stations to download ringtones, music and games; burn CDs; or surf the Internet. Four synchronized LCD monitors – one at each corner – display branded videos, promotional offers and manufacturer commercials.

And an interactive device lets customers test-drive featured products. When a product is lifted from its pedestal, a sensor triggers the overhead monitor to break from the loop and deliver a short module with product features. Based on positive results, 30 more stores or kiosks are planned nationwide.

CLIENT
Lifestyle Ventures LLC, New York

ARCHITECT AND DESIGN
EWI Worldwide, Livonia, Mich. – Sandor Koteles, creative director; David Urbiel, designer

OUTSIDE DESIGN CONSULTANT
Lifestyle Ventures LLC, New York (graphics and design concept)

FLOORING
Kährs International, Inc., Altamonte Springs, Fla.

FURNITURE
Jaymar, Terrebonne, Que.

LAMINATE
Arpa Industriale S.P.A., Via Piumati, Italy

LIGHTING
Juno Lighting Group, Des Plaines, Ill.

MERCHANDISING
Marlite, Dover, Ohio; Vanguard Products Group, Oldsmar, Fla.

SIGNAGE AND GRID CEILING
Townsend Neon, Rockwood, Mich.

PHOTOGRAPHY
Laszlo Regos, Berkley, Mich.

CRYSTAL RESTAURANT/LOUNGE

The new Crystal restaurant/lounge is situated at the pinnacle of the Royal Ontario Museum's new five-story aluminum-and-glass addition by architect Daniel Libeskind. The interior design is an extension of the bold, angular architecture (no right angles here).

The high-contrast space boasts a white interior punctuated by an ebony floor; ivory leather seating; sette backs in bleached anigre; and tabletops, feature walls and metal fittings in acid-etched mirror bronze. A sculptural glass screen separates the entry corridor from the black granite bar. And architecturally driven light fixtures include diagonally mounted light sticks over the bar and "slashes" of light in the walls and ceiling.

CLIENT
Royal Ontario Museum, Toronto

DESIGN
II BY IV Design Associates Inc., Toronto – Dan Menchions and Keith Rushbrook, partners; Grace Eng and Tanya Yeung, senior designers; Wilson Lau, intermediate designer; Kevin Bongard, senior project manager

ARCHITECT/PRIME CONSULTANT
Bregman + Hamann Architects, Toronto

BASE BUILDING ARCHITECT
Studio Daniel Libeskind, New York, with Bregman + Hamann Architects, Toronto

GENERAL CONTRACTOR
Vanbots Construction Corp., Markham, Ont.

OUTSIDE DESIGN CONSULTANTS
Bregman + Hamann Architects, Toronto (joint venture architect); Halsall, Toronto (structural engineer); The Mitchell Partnership, Willowdale, Ont. (mechanical engineer); Mulvey + Banani Intl. Inc., Toronto (electrical engineer); Valcoustics, Richmond Hill, Ont. (acoustics); Leber Rubes Inc., Toronto (life safety); The Restaurant Associates, New York (operator)

GLASS SCULPTURE
Jeff Goodman, Toronto

FLOORING
W Studio, Toronto (area carpets); Armstrong, Lancaster, Pa.; Hartco, Lancaster, Pa. (hardwood)

FURNITURE
Keilhauer, Toronto (lounge furniture); ISA Intl., Toronto (custom dining chairs); DJ McCrae, Toronto (custom furniture)

LIGHTING
Eurolite, Toronto (bar pendant lights)

PHOTOGRAPHY
David Whittaker, Toronto

40 CARROTS

After 32 years at Bloomingdale's metro level, 40 Carrots got an upgrade that included a vertical move, expanded seating and an interior transformation. Bright, modern and inviting, the new space generously incorporates garden-inspired colors and materials.

Natural materials include reconstituted bamboo flooring in the seating area, porcelain tile flooring in high-traffic areas (such as takeaway) and reconstituted wood seating. White textured walls add visual interest and a break from the colorful interior. And the columns' custom, striped wallcovering was translated into placemats and printed matter that give the restaurant a new graphic signature.

CLIENT
Macy's Inc., Cincinnati

RETAIL TEAM
Bloomingdale's, New York – Jack Hruska, senior vice president, visual merchandising and store design; Shan DiNapoli, vice president, store design; Diane Koester

DESIGN/ARCHITECTURE
Mancini Duffy, New York – Evangelo Dascal, principal and account director; Ed Calabrese, creative director; Lisa Contreras, resource director; Geoffrey Prisco, architect; George Winsperer, technical; Karen Kornbau

GENERAL CONTRACTOR
Piece Management, New Hyde Park, N.Y.

OUTSIDE DESIGN CONSULTANTS
Doug Russell Lighting, New York (lighting)

FURNITURE
Wesnic Furniture, Jacksonville, Fla.

TILE
Stone Source, New York; American Olean, Dallas; Dal-Tile, Dallas

PHOTOGRAPHY
Robert Mitra, New York

INNOVATION AWARD FOR GRAPHICS

CITRINE

Citrine is a new-concept fast-casual restaurant that emphasizes fresh ingredients and culinary exploration. The client, Safeway Inc., viewed the venue as an opportunity to extend its food expertise outside the grocery-store arena and test its products in their "final" form.

The bright, contemporary space communicates "food as passport," "food as fashion" and "food as lifestyle" through bold graphics, clear type and distinct culinary zones. For example, the restaurant includes a wine bar, a Dash & Dine area with a separate entrance and a display kitchen. Stainless-steel equipment and materials lend a high-end kitchen feel, while a large community table adds a homespun touch.

CLIENT
Safeway, Inc., Pleasanton, Calif. – Eric Quick, formerly president of SRG; Loret Carbone, president and COO, SRG; Jeff Anderson, vice president, culinary exploration, SRG

DESIGN/ARCHITECTURE
WD Partners, Dublin, Ohio – Lee Peterson, vice president, creative services; Bob Welty, director, integrated prototype solutions; Mike Corbett, client program manager; Keith Jasinski, architecture/engineering project manager; Eric Daniel, prototype director; Christopher Michaels, Sarah McDaniel, Randy Moore and Brian Bucher, prototype designers; Rob Turner, 3D studio manager

OUTSIDE DESIGN CONSULTANT
Rodgers Townsend, St. Louis (SRG ad agency)

METALWORK
Cozmyk Enterprises, Columbus, Ohio

FURNITURE
Avis Furniture, Kansas City, Mo. (booths and banquettes); Commercial Furniture Group, St. Louis (table bases); Gordon Intl., New York (chairs); American Trading Co., Fallsington, Pa. (patio table bases); TSE Restaurant Fixtures, Toledo, Ohio (bar stools); Knoll Studio, Columbus, Ohio (patio chairs); Tim O'Neil and Associates, Columbus, Ohio (dining table base, cantilevered bracket)

MILLWORK
Wisconsin Built, Deerfield, Wis.

SIGNAGE/GRAPHICS
P&R Group, Chicago (interior signage); Tork Inc., Columbus, Ohio (oven logo); CenSource, Anaheim, Calif. (exterior signage)

PHOTOGRAPHY
Kingmond Young, San Francisco

dash & dine

enjoy umbria with
a little edamame.

PIZZAEXPRESS

PizzaExpress has opened its latest restaurant in Brighton, U.K., a town with a vibrant arts and a collection of independent retailers.

JHP, the London design consultancy, created the pizza shop to be a reflection of the seaside town's free-spirited nature. Its personality projects a colorful, social setting through bright pink furnishings and neon blue LEDs. Timber cladding on the ceiling, walls and columns adds an earthy, natural feel.

Forget about cracking open a cold one here. Each white marble-topped table is set with wine glasses, silverware and a single flower centerpiece for a sophisticated flair.

For a lively atmosphere, designers left the food-preparation area visible to patrons. Chefs toss dough in the air and prepare toppings on a white marble pizza counter.

CLIENT
PizzaExpress, Middlesex, U.K.

DESIGN
JHP, London – David Rook, designer

ARCHITECT
Butler Associates, Epsom, U.K.

GENERAL CONTRACTOR
Metz Construction, Surbiton, U.K.

TILES
Strata Tiles Ltd., Surrey, U.K.

TIMBER CLADDING
Luxalon, Staffordshire, U.K.

SIGNAGE
Technical Signs, Watford, U.K.

FURNITURE
Kudos Interiors, Surrey, U.K.

PHOTOGRAPHY
Sara Louise Ramsay, London

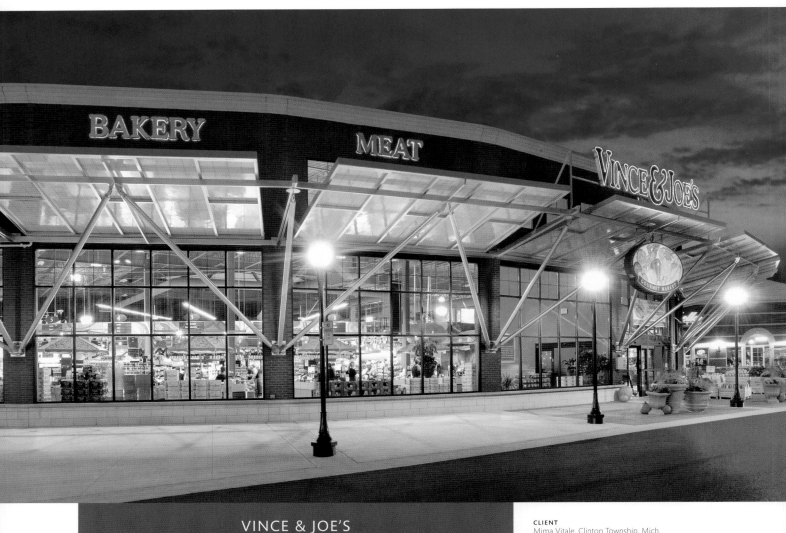

VINCE & JOE'S

Vince & Joe's is a specialty food shop rooted in a passion for food, heirloom recipes and diverse specialty products in an unpretentious setting. The challenge for designers was transferring those values into a space double the size of the previous one.

The bowed-glass storefront connects the interior and exterior, which has a large plaza for outdoor displays and seating. Merchandise fixtures on the interior radiate from the center, service departments are arrayed around the perimeter, and specialty offerings on islands invite a sense of discovery. Exposed ceilings, track lighting and concrete floors help put the emphasis on the colorful products.

CLIENT
Mima Vitale, Clinton Township, Mich.

DESIGN
Marco Retail Group, Northville, Mich. – Nicholas Giammarco, president

ARCHITECT
Quinlan Associates, St. Clair Shores, Mich.

GENERAL CONTRACTOR
JN Construction, Clinton Township, Mich.

DÉCOR
Shaw & Slavsky, Detroit

FABRIC
Designtex, New York; Architex, Sarasota, Fla.; Donghia, Mt. Vernon, N.Y.

FIXTURES
Lozier, Omaha, Neb.; Group Four, South Bend, Ind.; Hussman, Bridgeton, Mo.

FLOORING
Beaver Tile & Stone, Grand Rapids, Mich., and Virginia Tile Co., Livonia, Mich. (tile); The Matworks, Beltsville, Md.

LAMINATES
Pionite/Panolam Industries, Shelton, Conn.; Chemetal, Easthampton, Mass.; Interlam, Claudville, Va.; Formica Corp., Cincinnati

LIGHTING
Juno Lighting, Des Plaines, Ill.; Alfa, city, state; Amerlux, Fairfield, N.J.; Enzo Altre Di Verduno Collection, New York; LBL Lighting/ Design Galleries, Chicago; Lithonia, Conyers, Ga.

PAINT
Benjamin Moore & Co., Montvale, N.J.; Sherwin-Williams, Cleveland

SPECIAL FINISHES
Avonite, Mississauga, Ont.; Zodiac, Sterling Heights, Mich.

PHOTOGRAPHY
DK Photographic Illustration, New Baltimore, Mich.

JOE'S PRODUCE

Joe's Produce began as a small roadside stand in Livonia, Mich. In 1967, the stand became a store. And after years of selling produce from that same store, Joe's was ready for an update.

Marco Retail Group (Northville Mich.) decided a fresh, open-air environment with natural accents like stone and stained concrete would best fit Joe's fresh offerings.

The store is bathed in natural light from a wall of windows. Modern, rounded lighting fixtures accent produce cases and fixtures.

Earthy colors in the stone tiles and flooring provide a warm backdrop.

CLIENT
Joe Maiorana, Livonia, Mich.

DESIGN
Marco Retail Group, Northville, Mich. – Nick Giammarco, president; Andrew Bourdon, designer

ARCHITECT
Kevin Hart & Associates, Birmingham, Mich.

AWNING
Signature Awning, Livonia, Mich.

FABRIC
Sunbrella, Maharam, Mich.

FLOORING
Increte, Odessa, Fla.; Marca Corona, Sassuolo, Italy; C-S Group, Lebanon, N.J.; Constantine Commercial LLC, Calhoun, Ga.; Johnsonite, Chagrin Falls, Ohio

TILE
Schluter Systems, Plattsburgh, N.Y.; United States Ceramic Tile Co., Miami; Genessee Ceramic, Troy, Mich.

EXTERIOR FINISHES
Stone Tiles Intl., Toronto; KalWall Corp., Manchester, N.H.

SPECIAL FINISHES
Ven Tec, Wixom, Mich.

PHOTOGRAPHY
Don Kurek Photography, Northville, Mich.

LANDMARK SUPERMARKET

Challenges abounded when designing the Landmark Supermarket, part of the new Landmark Department Store in Manila. For one, a series of structural columns were reinforced with large, low-hanging armatures, lowering the ceiling height to 11 feet. To open things up, light-colored, floating planes are suspended below the dark, exposed ceiling and the columns are wrapped with images of local fruits and flowers.

To reduce energy costs, efficient metal-halide and fluorescent light fixtures illuminate vertical surfaces and key displays, while overall lighting levels are kept low. And gypsum and solid-surface acrylic are used instead of wood, which is highly restricted in the Philippines.

CLIENT
Landmark, Manila, Philippines – David Go, head of construction; Arlene Encinas, senior project manager; Noel Tolin, head of engineering; Norman Manalo, head of store planning

DESIGN/ARCHITECTURE
Hugh A. Boyd Architects, Monclair, N.J. – Hugh Boyd, principal; A. Henderson Boyd, JoAnn Montero

GENERAL CONTRACTOR
Constech, Quezon City, Philippines

OUTSIDE DESIGN CONSULTANTS
The Lighting Practice, Philadelphia (lighting); Leslie Evans Design, Cape Elizabeth, Maine (graphic design); GRA Architects, Clark, N.J. (presentation graphics); Susan Roberts, Athens, Ga. (colors and bowl designs); The Landmark, Manila, Philippines (construction)

CHECKOUTS
Pan-Oston Sdn. Bhd., Malaysia

FLOORING
Architectural Materials Supplies Trading Co., Hong Kong

FURNITURE
Ramler Contract, Victoria, Australia (tables and chairs)

LIGHTING
Ping Hao Lighting, Zhongshan, China

METAL DISPLAY UNITS/SHOPPING CARTS
Target Display, Manila, Philippines

REFRIGERATED DISPLAY CASES
Hussmann Tempcool PTE, Singapore

STAINLESS-STEEL DISPLAYS
FabTech, Valenzuela, Philippines

PHOTOGRAPHY
Toto Labrador, 2nd Storey Studios, Quezon City, Philippines

INNOVATION AWARD FOR STORE PLANNING

WHOLE FOODS MARKET

To create an eco-industrial store that simultaneously honors the environment and its historic South Loop location, designers minimized materials and used resources wisely for the new 53,000-square-foot Whole Foods Market in Chicago. For example, renewable, local, recycled, low-VOC and certified wood materials are used throughout the store.

Fluorescent, ceramic metal-halide and natural lighting increase energy efficiency. And even a signage system fabricated from cork, thermoplastic, bamboo and SCS-certified particleboard educates consumers about sustainability.

CLIENT
Whole Foods Market, Chicago – Christine Wiegand, Midwest design coordinator

DESIGN/ARCHITECTURE
Heights Venture Architects LLP, Houston – Stephen Jovicich, partner-in-charge; Amanda Tullos, designer/LEED consultant; Thea Luong, project manager/designer

GENERAL CONTRACTOR
Osman Construction Co., Arlington Heights, Ill.

OUTSIDE DESIGN CONSULTANTS
Clive Samuels Associates, Princeton, N.J. (engineer); Jack O'Conner, Commercial, Design Systems, Portland, Ore. (interior design and branding)

LIGHTING
Western Extralite, Maryland Heights, Mo.

MILLWORK
Capital Wood Products, St. Paul, Minn.

MATERIALS
Fireclay Tile, San Jose, Calif.; Purebond, Portland, Ore.; Marmoleum, Hazleton, Pa.; 3form, Salt Lake City; ICI Paints, Strongsville, Ohio; Ozinga, Chicago; Eurostone, Chicago; Retroplate, Provo, Utah; Georgia Pacific, Atlanta; Natural Cork, Chicago

PHOTOGRAPHY
Advanced Technologies Inc., Houston, and Heights Venture Architects LLP, Houston

We sell the highest quality natural and organic products available.

We satisfy and delight our customers.

We care about Team Member happiness and excellence.

We create wealth through profits and growth.

We care about our communities and our environment.

and safe to eat.

We feature foods free from artificial preservatives, colors, flavors, sweeteners and hydrogenated fats.

We seek out and promote organically grown foods.

We are passionate about great tasting food and the pleasure of sharing it with each other.

We provide food and nutritional products that support health and well being.

CHEVROLET

1252 XE

CITY MARKET

City Market, a high-end supermarket in Magno Centro, Mexico, taps the senses to evoke the feel of an elegant European gourmet market. To draw attention in a challenging location – in the basement of a mall – a bright, open glass façade with a black-granite and steel frame offers clear sightlines into the store.

Once inside, strong colors and graphics highlight specialty areas for food, wine and cooking demonstrations. And stainless-steel fixtures and displays, combined with warm woods, colorful glass mosaics and decorative pendants, imbue a soft yet contemporary attitude.

CLIENT
Comercial Mexicana, Mexico City
DESIGN
Pavlik Design Team, Ft. Lauderdale, Fla.
ARCHITECT
Ht Arquitectos, S.A. de C.V. Mexico City
GENERAL CONTRACTOR/FLOORING/WALLCOVERINGS/MATERIALS
Grupo VYG, Mexico City
CEILINGS
Decoraciones Nueva Era S.A. de C.V., Mexico City
FURNITURE
Grupo STOR, Mexico City
LIGHTING
Electroproyectos y Construccion S.A. de C.V., Mexico City
SIGNAGE/GRAPHICS
Formacryl de Mexico, Mexico City
PHOTOGRAPHY
Dana Hoff Photography, Jupiter, Fla.

GO FRESH

Go Fresh, a new-concept convenience store in London, uses graphics, color and lighting to create a fun and inviting environment for commuters. Taking advantage of the store's unique location – underneath the barrel vaulting of a bridge – an arched keyhole entrance was built to frame the unit and draw curious customers in. Finished in a high-gloss white lacquer, the brightly polished entrance also contrasts nicely with the rough, exposed station walls.

Signage around the store's perimeter features the Go Fresh logo prominently, architectural track lighting creates visual zones within the space and an arched ceiling adds to the open feel.

CLIENT
Noel Smith, Dublin, Ireland – Fiona Walsh

DESIGN/ARCHITECTURE
Douglas\Wallace Architects, Dublin, Ireland – Samantha Gates, designer/project leader; Adrian Lambe, designer

GENERAL CONTRACTOR
EMC Contracting, Dundalk, Ireland

OUTSIDE DESIGN CONSULTANTS
Design Factory, Dublin, Ireland (graphics)

SHOPFITTING
A.M.G. Fit-Out, Kildare, Ireland

SIGNAGE
E. Tapley Installation Ltd., Dublin, Ireland

PHOTOGRAPHY
Courtesy of Design Factory, Dublin, Ireland

WOW

Convenience stores are gaining in popularity in this time-crunched, grab-and-go culture. They're also getting special design attention. And WOW, a Detroit c-store and gas station chain owned by Atlas Oil Co. is no exception.

Offering more fresh options, such as produce, flowers, prepared foods and deli selections, WOW features a cheery, energized environment with stylized graphics and warm, sun-baked colors to add visual interest. Designers at D|Fab developed a sunflower icon and the "We Offer Wonderful" tagline used on the building façade, pumps and gas canopy. The sunflower image is reinterpreted throughout the store on surfaces surrounding prepared foods, wayfinding signage and wall stencils.

Red, yellow and fiery orange mix with accents of sage and blue coloring signage, walls and the ceiling. Granite counters and dark wood millwork provide an upscale feel.

CLIENT/GENERAL CONTRACTOR
Atlas Oil Co., Taylor, Mich.

DESIGN
D|Fab Inc., Madison Heights, Mich. – Gregory Geralds, president; Tony Camilletti, vp; Paul Hilpert, graphic designer; Gretchen Heinle, design studio manager; Patty Price Frey, account executive

ARCHITECT
G.A.V. & Associates Inc., Farmington Hills, Mich.

DÉCOR, ARCHITECTURAL ELEMENTS, GRAPHICS
D|Fab Inc., Madison Heights, Mich. – Jessie Roberts, operations director; David Dunaj, engeineering director

FIXTURES
Shopco USA Inc., Houston; Convenience Store Equipment Sales, Livonia, Mich.

MILLWORK
Creative Store Fixtures, Warren, Mich.

TILE
Virginia Tile, Livonia, Mich.

LIGHTING
Juno Lighting, Des Plaines, Ill.

PHOTOGRAPHY
Tony Camilletti, D|Fab Inc., Madison Heights, Mich.

MOTOROLA M-LAB

Located in an indoor role-playing theme park in Florida, Motorola's M-Lab playfully introduces children to technology careers and the Motorola brand. The 1,200-square-foot space mimics a submersible vehicle and uses an interactive video game to engage kids.

After entering through a glowing aluminum façade, children encounter several zones. For example, in Mission Control, kids don white lab coats and go on a mission to find and tag new fish species. Sights, sounds, and smells raise the energy level until their mission is accomplished. Raised-rubber flooring, high-gloss metal walls and fixtures and video screen portholes contribute to the learning-laboratory feel.

CLIENT
Motorola, New York

DESIGN
Gensler, Santa Monica, Calif. – Russell Banks, creative director; Deanna Goodwin, design director; Banning Rowles and Michael White, senior designers; Michelle Wallace, production manager; Chris Florin, environmental graphic design technical director

ARCHITECT
The Madfis Group, Ft. Lauderdale, Fla.

GENERAL CONTRACTOR
MC2, Chestnut Ridge, N.Y.

OUTSIDE DESIGN CONSULTANTS
ImaginEngine, Framingham, Mass. (game designer); MC2, Chestnut Ridge, N.Y. (audio/visual, lighting, technical assistance)

PHOTOGRAPHY
Adrian Wilson, New York

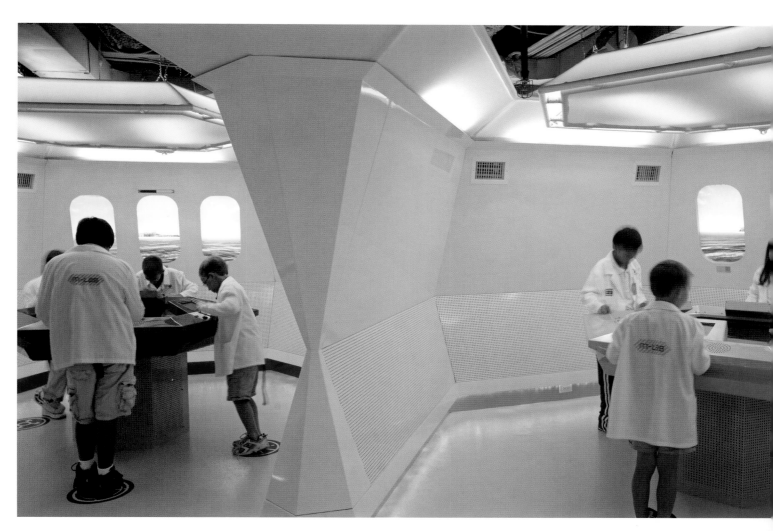

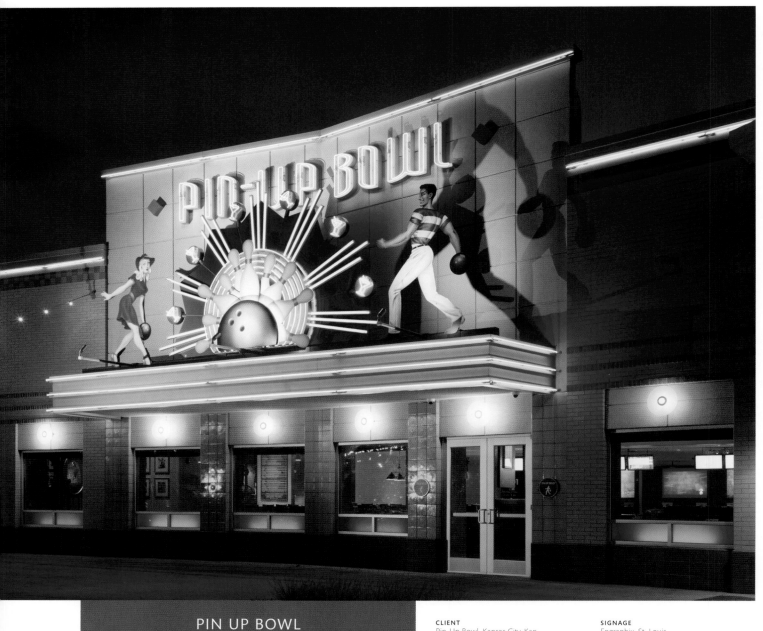

PIN UP BOWL

Bowling alley and martini lounge, Pin-Up Bowl is just one of the entertainment options in The Legends at Village West, a new development in Kansas City, Kan. To combine a martini lounge and a bowling alley, the client wanted a retro feel, but not one that would imitate any single style or era.

So Kiku Obata & Co. created a design concept with a fun, relaxed, unpretentious vibe.

Art deco became the inspiration for Pin-Up Bowl, from its retro-chic, neon blue façade to its swanky red and yellow lounge area. Elements such as contemporary graphics and modern materials provide a contrast to the deco style.

CLIENT
Pin-Up Bowl, Kansas City, Kan.

DESIGN/ARCHITECTURE
Kiku Obata & Co., St. Louis – Kiku Obata, president; Kevin Flynn, Dennis Hyland, Rich Nelson, Lisa Bollmann, Jim Redington, Sarah Royal, designers

GENERAL CONTRACTOR
Phoenix Building Group, Stilwell, Kan.

OUTSIDE DESIGN CONSULTANTS
Red Development, Kansas City, Mo. (developer); William Tao & Associates, Kansas City, Kan. (MEP engineer); Page McNaghten Associates, Kansas City, Kan. (structural engineer)

KITCHEN, BAR, FURNITURE
Ford Hotel Supply Co., St. Louis

AUDIO/VISUAL
Technical Productions, St. Louis

SIGNAGE
Engraphix, St. Louis

MILLWORK
Woodbyrne, St. Louis

BOWLING LANES AND EQUIPMENT
Brunswick, Lake Forest, Ill.

ARTWORK
Gallery Framing, St. Louis

FLOORING
Lees Carpets, Kennesaw, Ga.; Johnsonite, Chagrin Falls, Ohio

LIGHTING
Cooper Lighting, Peachtree City, Ga.; Eureka Lighting, Montreal; Ardee Lighting, Shelby, N.C.; Tech Lighting, Skokie, Ill.; Lucifer Lighting. San Antonio, Texas; Lighting Services Inc, Stony Point, N.Y.; Day-Brite, Tupelo, Mo.

PHOTOGRAPHY
XXXXXX getting photo form

PETER MARK

CLIENT
Peter Mark, Dublin, Ireland
INTERIOR DESIGNERS
Douglas|Wallace Architects, Dublin, Ireland –
Brian Jennings, project director; Tarik Abood,
project leader; Aoife Rhattigan, designer
GENERAL CONTRACTOR
JF McCue, Antrim, Ireland
OUTSIDE DESIGN CONSULTANTS
Austin Butler, Dublin, Ireland (graphics);
Academy Signs, Dublin, Ireland (signage);
McKenna Pearce Practice Structural Engineers,
Dublin, Ireland (structural engineer)
JOINERY SUPPLIER
K.G. Interiors, Coalisland, Ireland
PHOTOGRAPHY
Gerry O'Leary, Dublin, Ireland

To revamp Peter Mark's image from classic up-market salon to urban salon/retail venue, the design team was tasked with creating a retail store within a salon that would showcase Peter Mark's hair-care knowledge and appeal to a younger demographic.

The expanded salon puts an emphasis on product purchases, with recommendation panels incorporated into the fixtures. An interchangeable system helps customers make choices based on the stylists' personal experiences. And designers incorporated bold red and orange graphics, red resin screens and edgy graphics on the walls to infuse a funky-chic feel to the primarily white space.

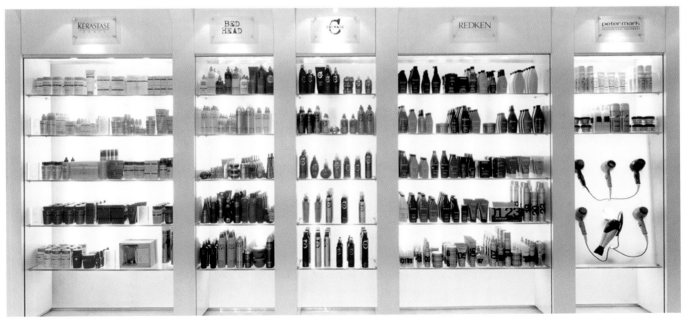

MR. CLEAN PERFORMANCE CAR WASH

Mr. Clean has been branching out big time – the Procter & Gamble brand's sales have tripled in the last five years to more than $400 million with the launch of such product extensions as the Mr. Clean Magic Eraser and Mr. Clean AutoDry home car-wash product. Now, the Cincinnati-based consumer products giant has turned the brand and its bald-headed icon into a retail experience at the Mr. Clean Performance Car Wash, created by Design Forum.

Based on consumer feedback it gathered, Design Forum concluded the Mr. Clean Performance Car Wash should "be loaded with amenities and be especially focused on the female customer, who we discovered often feels uncomfortable in traditional car washes," says Scott Jeffrey, Design Forum's chief creative officer. So the experience is designed to be clean, bright, friendly and safe. The car wash's visual centerpiece is a blue canopy that's designed to communicate performance and highlight the moment when the car is "magically clean."

"We wanted the canopy arches to be contemporary and simple," says Jeffrey. "They are impactful from a distance and they differentiate. They really become an architectural icon for the brand."

CLIENT
Procter & Gamble, Cincinnati

DESIGN/ARCHITECTURE
Design Forum, Dayton, Ohio – Scott Jeffrey, chief creative officer

GENERAL CONTRACTOR
GLR, Dayton, Ohio

CEILING
Armstrong World Industries Inc., Lancaster, Pa.

FIXTURES
RTC, Rolling Meadows, Ill.

FLOORING
Atmosphere Rubber Flooring from To Market, Oklahoma City, Okla.; Lonseal, Carson, Calif.

FURNITURE
Turnstone by Steelcase, Grand Rapids, Mich.; Brayton Intl. by Steelcase, Grand Rapids, Mich.; INDX Designs, Greensboro, N.C.; Cabot Wren, Hickory, N.C.

GRAPHICS
LSI Graphic Solutions Plus, North Canton, Ohio

PAINT FINISHES
ICI Paints, Cleveland

PLASTIC LAMINATES
Pionite Decorative Surfaces/Panolam, Auburn, Maine; Abet Laminati, Englewood, N.J.; Wilsonart Intl., Temple, Texas

PHOTOGRAPHY
Bob Winner, Winner Photography, Dayton, Ohio

HIQ

CLIENT
HiQ, Nottingham, U.K.

DESIGN
Fitch Design Consultants, London – Simon Moriarty,
design studio director; Sam Stone, design director;
Leigh Chandler and Dominic Keighley, designers

GENERAL CONTRACTOR
Colin Robotham, London

PHOTOGRAPHY
Tom Dunkley, London

Honesty and trust aren't two words that typically come to mind when thinking of car-repair companies. The technical jargon and the high prices, coupled with the fact that most consumers aren't familiar with the workings of cars, can leave them feeling anxious.

For HiQ, Britain's quick-service car-care brand, Fitch's London office faced the challenge of alleviating that anxiety through an environment that reflects the service retailer's strong customer-focused ethos.

An overall blue and black color scheme with pink and green accents marks a departure from traditional colors associated with car-repair providers and differentiates HiQ from its competitors. Glass walls communicate openness and allow customers to see onto the garage floor. Simple signage states, "We promise that we won't carry out unnecessary work ever," and upholds the retailer's mantra of top-notch, honest service.

INFINITI RETAIL ENVIRONMENT DESIGN INITIATIVE

To establish Infiniti firmly in the luxury automotive segment in Korea, the new six-story Infiniti dealership in Seoul attracts high-end customers from the outside in. A curved-glass storefront takes visual cues from the Infiniti logo, while the interior design has a boutique hotel vibe.

The first-floor lobby and mezzanine-level lounge offer comfortable seating and amenities for customers waiting for service, and the gallery showrooms display new cars dramatically against the backdrop of Seoul's skyline. Natural finishes, clean-lined furniture, custom fixtures and luminous lighting extend the well-appointed aesthetic and convey the brand's dual emphasis on technology and design.

CLIENT
Nissan North America Inc., Gardena, Calif. – Peter Bossis, senior manager

DESIGN
Lippincott, New York – Ken Roberts, CEO; Peter Dixon, senior partner/creative director; Fabian Diaz, partner; Pauline Young, senior associate; Soenghie Lee, associate

ARCHITECT
SL&A International Inc., Seoul, Korea

GENERAL CONTRACTOR
Yoongang, Seoul, Korea

OUTSIDE DESIGN CONSULTANTS
J+B Studios, Seoul, Korea (regional lighting consultant); Store Lighting Systems, Great Neck, N.Y. (overall lighting concept)

CARPET
Bentley Prince Street, New York

FABRIC
Maharam, New York

LEATHER
Cortina Leathers, New York

PAINT
Benjamin Moore & Co., Montvale, N.J.

SOLID-SURFACE
DuPont, Wilmington, Del.

STONE TILE
Stone Source, New York

PHOTOGRAPHY
Robert Polidori, New York

ALLSTEEL CANADIAN SHOWROOM

Allsteel Inc. wanted to display its line of workplace furniture to Toronto's design community in an inspiring setting. The Boiler House in the former Toronto Carpet Factory building filled that bill, with its 60-foot ceilings, leaded glass windows and exposed brick walls.

Designers from figure3 blended the old and the new throughout the three-level space in Toronto's historic Liberty Village. The reception area, for example, features a round guest seating area housed in the building's original smokestack, while on the space's upper level, visitors traverse the factory's original hardwood floor to get to a glass-sheathed conference room that sits on a cantilevered platform.

CLIENT
Allsteel Inc., Muscatine, Iowa – Timothy Smith, vp, resource center development

DESIGN
figure3, Toronto – Allan Guinan and Christopher Wright, partners, Eric Yorath, senior team lead; Patrick Rechtorik, Steve Tsai, Jacinthe Koddo, project designers

CONSTRUCTION MANAGER
Rae Brother, Toronto

OUTSIDE DESIGN FIRMS
Jacques Whitford, Sheila Brown, Marham, Ont. (LEED accreditation); Duocom, Richmond Hill, Ont. (lighting); BGM Imaging, Toronto (graphics); Smith and Andersen, Toronto (electrical, communications, mechanical and lighting consultants)

ACRYLICS
Cyro, Parsippany, N.J.; 3form, Salt Lake City

FLOORING
Interface, Toronto; Safecoat, San Diego; Niagara Protective Coatings, Niagara Falls, Ont.

FURNITURE
Allsteel Inc., Muscatine, Iowa

LAMINATES
Wilsonart Intl. Inc., Temple, Texas

PAINTS
Benjamin Moore, Montvale, N.J.; ICI, Concord, Ont.; Sherwin Williams, Cleveland

PLASTIC LAMINATES
Formica, Cincinnati; Panolam, Shelton, Conn.

SOLID SURFACING
DuPont, Wilmington, Del.

STONE
Marble Trend, Toronto

TILE-TRIM THRESHOLDS
Schluter, St.-Laurent, Que.

TILE
VitroCeram, Toronto; Olympia Tile, Toronto

PHOTOGRAPHY
Richard Johnson Photography, Toronto

P&G BEAUTY EXHIBIT

CLIENT
The Procter & Gamble Co., Cincinnati – Beth Harlor, principal design manager, beauty & health; Lauren Thaman, associate director, beauty science

DESIGN
Anthem Worldwide, Cincinnati – John Carpenter, executive creative director; Jennifer O'Shea, associate creative director; Jennifer McKinley, senior account manager; Mike Vine, design director; Robin Horvath, designer; Kelly Lenzer, senior project manager

PHOTOGRAPHY
Daniela MacAdden, Buenos Aires, Argentina

The 3500-square-foot P&G Beauty exhibit at the World Congress of Dermatology in Buenos Aires, Argentina, was designed as an immersive, three-part experience that engaged visitors with a "beauty on the outside–innovation within" approach. Semitransparent walls, curved panels and a white palette infused with colorful graphics lent a bright, feminine look to the exhibit.

The Pre-Show Gallery featured beauty bars and interactive stations that illustrated innovations in skin care, hair care and brand technology. Curved display counters with graphic back walls and staffed consultants educated visitors in the Innovation Center. And in the Theater, plasma screens delivered 20-minute videos on the benefits of P&G Beauty.

LOOK FAB STUDIO

Open for four weeks in Toronto's Bloor Street shopping district, the 2400-square-foot Look Fab Studio invited visitors to explore P&G's beauty brands and products in a dynamic retail environment. Designers used an orchid as a visual metaphor and design cue for the graphics, fixtures, materials and flooring patterns.

The dramatic entrance featured a series of over-scaled, sweeping, stretched-fabric arches and hanging acrylic orbs filled with inspirational design cues. Inside, the unabashedly feminine design boasted tone-on-tone white cork flooring, acrylic seating and counters and walls with splashes of vivid pink. Curved graphic panels delineated beauty areas, while flowing banners reinforced P&G brands.

CLIENT
P&G Canada, Consumer Beauty Care, Toronto – Judi Hoffman, category brand manager; Sam Minardi, brand manager; Stephanie Couture, assistant business manager

DESIGN
Upshot, Chicago – Brian Priest, vice president, environmental design; Lisa Hurst, vice president, account management; Brooke Ward, account manager; Angie Taormina, art director; Kim Pacion, senior copywriter; Scott Irwin, production director; Erica Bletsch, production manager; Katy Gannon, production artist

ARCHITECT
Chandler Graham Architects & Designers, Toronto

FIXTURE MANUFACTURER/BUILDOUT/CONTRACTOR
The Taylor Group, Brampton, Ont.

OUTSIDE DESIGN CONSULTANTS
Jesslin Interiors, Scarborough, Ont. (construction); BOI Solutions, Centerville, Ohio (technology)

FLOORING
To Market, Oklahoma City, Okla.

PHOTOGRAPHY
Mark Steele, Columbus, Ohio

For more information on visual merchandising and store design, subscribe to:

Experience Retail Now

**Books on visual merchandising and store design
available from ST Media Group International:**

Aesthetics of Merchandising Presentation
Budget Guide to Retail Store Planning & Design
Complete Guide to Effective Jewelry Store Display
Feng Shui for Retailers
Retail Renovation
Retail Store Planning & Design Manual
Stores and Retail Spaces
Visual Merchandising
Visual Merchandising and Store Design Workbook

**To subscribe, order books or request a complete catalog
of related books and magazines, please contact:**

ST Media Group International Inc.
11262 Cornell Park Drive. | Cincinnati, Ohio 45242

p: 1.800.925.1110 or 513.421.2050
f: 513.421.5144 or 513.744.6999
e: books@stmediagroup.com
www.stmediagroup.com (ST Books)
www.vmsd.com (*VMSD* Magazine)
www.irdconline.com (International Retail Design Conference)